CÉSAR AVILÉS

BOW MASTERY

An Introduction to Bow Arm Awareness

www.StringOrchestraSheetMusic.com

Warning!

Unauthorized reproduction of this publication is prohibited
by federal law and subject to criminal prosecution.

The music in this book is completely original.
The selections were composed by César Avilés and published by "Titoshack Publishers".

More from this publisher

Third Position Studies for Violin: In the Style of Film Music (Volume 1)

Third Position Studies for Violin: In the Style of Film Music (Volume 2)

©2019 by César Avilés
For further information please visit: www.stringorchestrasheetmusic.com

Introduction

Violin playing is a complex art that requires great control of an ample range of movements. The careful training of those movements helps violinists gain the ability to express themselves through music. Too often, students disregard the bow arm and focus exclusively on their left hand/arm training. This book is designed to balance this inadequacy.

Bow Mastery will prompt students to focus on bowing patterns, soundpoint selections, and bow placement (upper half, middle, and lower half). At the same time, students will be compelled to experiment with bow speed and hand pressure in order to obtain an even sound.

Additionally, I urge the student to study the full collection of Sevcik's *School of Bowing Technique op. 2* and the *40 Variations op. 3* so that the learning process can be accelerated.

It is crucial to be patient. As with every aspect of violin playing, bow arm technique is an infinite journey. It is my wish that *Bow Mastery* inspires students to master this art, and that it keeps them motivated to learn and grow as a musician, performer, and ultimately as an artist.

"It's not what we do once in a while that shapes our lives. It's what we do consistently."
— Anthony Robbins

Online Resources

First, go to: www.stringorchestrasheetmusic.com/violin

Click on: Bow Mastery Resources

Enter the password located on the last page of this book.

Once on the page, you will be able to download:

- MP3s of all pieces recorded on violin.
- MP3s of the accompaniment tracks.
- The accompaniment lead sheet (chords) for the whole book in PDF format.
- Other recommended material

Thank you for supporting my work!

César Avilés

avilesmusik@gmail.com

Recorded Accompaniment

- The accompaniment tracks will count in **one bar** before the pieces start.

- In the event of having **rests** in the first bar of the piece, you will hear **one bar counted in plus the additional rests of bar one.**

Content

The etudes in **Bow Mastery** are based on the following selected variations from **Sevcik's School of Bowing Technique op. 2 (Book 1)**.

Page	Bow Mastery Etudes	Sevcik's op. 2 Book 1
2	One	Ex.3 Variation 1,3,4,8
4	Two	Ex.3 Variation 16,17
6	Three	Ex.3 Variation 25,26
8	Four	Ex.3 variation 40,51
10	Five	Ex.5 Variation 1,2,7
12	Six	Ex.5 Variation 16,17,28
14	Seven	Ex.4 Variation 70,71,72
16	Eight	---
18	Nine	Ex.5 Variation 67,70,71
20	Ten	Ex.5 Variation 48,56
22	Eleven A	Ex.5 Variation 81,82,84
23	Eleven B	Ex.5 Variation 89
24	Twelve	Ex.5 Variation 98
26	Thirteen	Ex.6 Variation 6,7,8,9,10
28	Fourteen	Ex.7 Variation 1,2,3,4,5,6
30	Fifteen	Ex.7 Variation 42,46
32	Sixteen	Ex.13 Variation 1,2,3,7,8,9
34	Seventeen	Ex.15 Variation 1,2,3,4
36	Eighteen	Ex.16 Variation 1,2,3,4
38	Nineteen	Ex.17 Variation 80,81,83
40	Twenty	Ex.5 Variation 18,19,20,21

ABBREVIATIONS AND SYMBOLS

WB = WHOLE BOW

LH = LOWER HALF

1/2   1/2

UH = UPPER HALF

1/2   1/2

FR = AT THE FROG (HEEL)

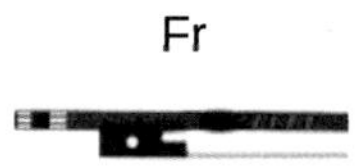

PT = AT THE POINT (TIP)

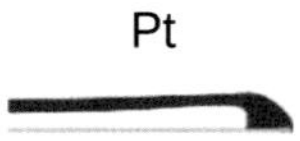

M = MIDDLE OF THE BOW

⊓ = DOWN BOW

V = UP BOW

• = STACCATO

— = BROADLY DETACHED

SIMILE = SIMILAR

STICKER PLACEMENT

GREEN 🟢 WHOLE BOW

BLUE 🔵 TIP AND FROG (HEEL)

RED 🔴 UPPER HALF AND LOWER HALF

SOUNDPOINTS

Soundpoints (or contact points) are like parallel road lanes on which the bow may travel. Students must deliberately choose a particular soundpoint depending on the sonority, character, and expressiveness of the emotions they want to convey.

Begin exploring this concept by practicing the recommended soundpoints in each etude. These are marked with **circled numbers**.

Intentionally Blank

BOW MASTERY

ONE

♩ = 90

C.A.

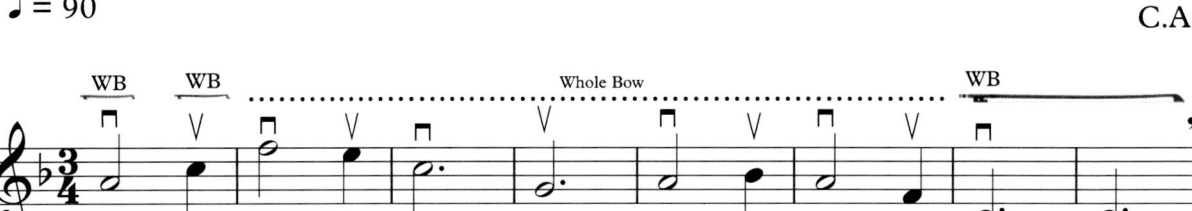
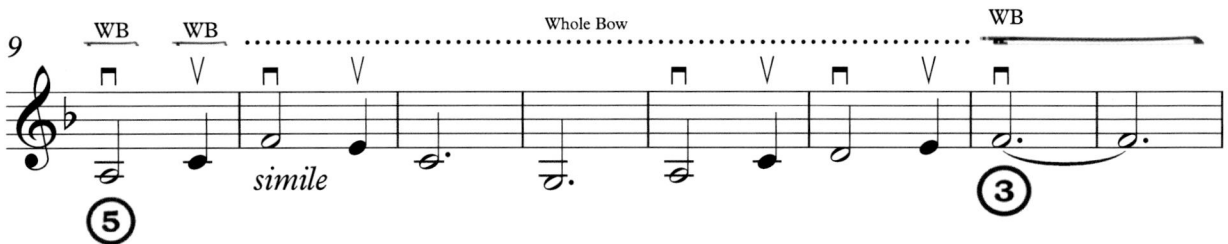
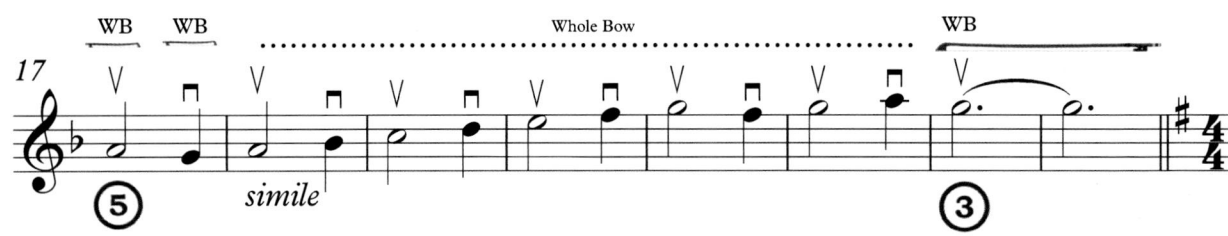
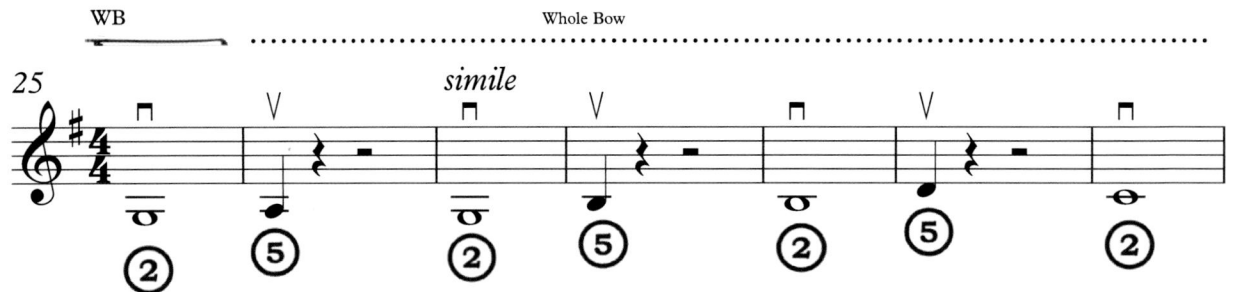

3

Two

♩ = 90

C.A.

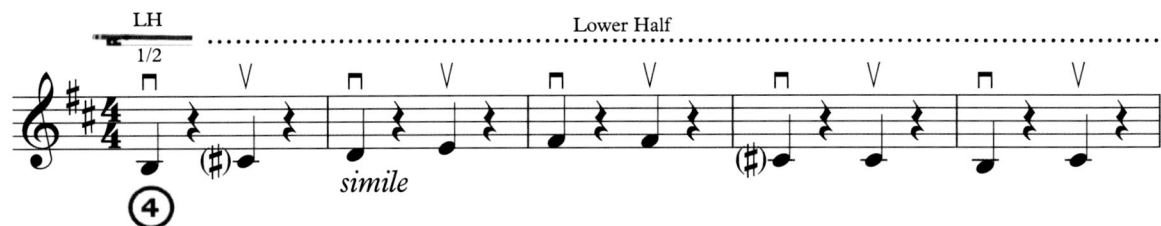
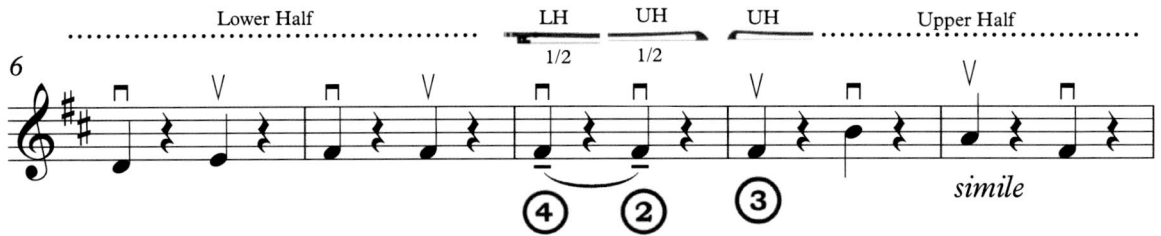
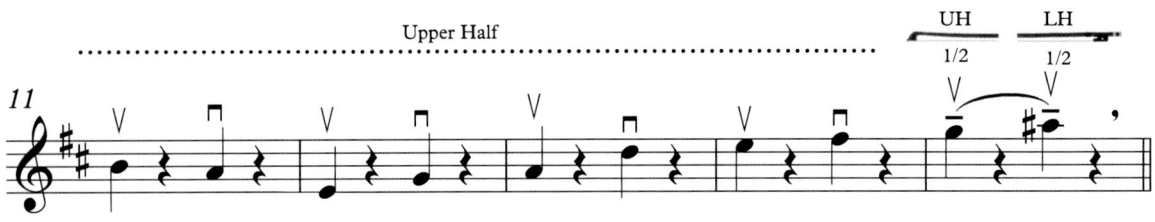
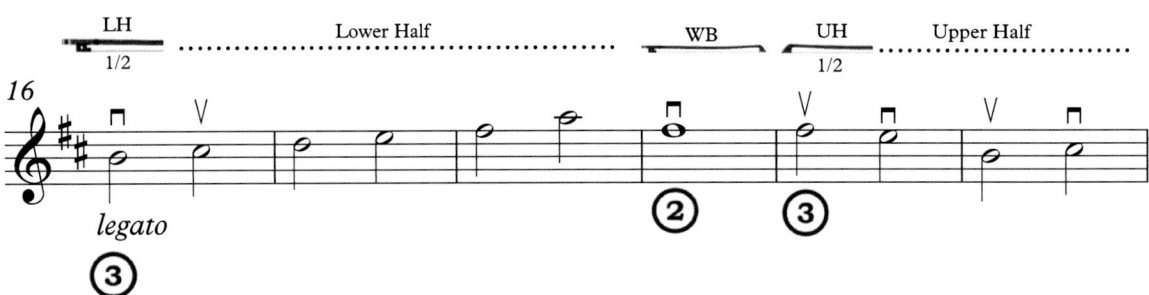

5

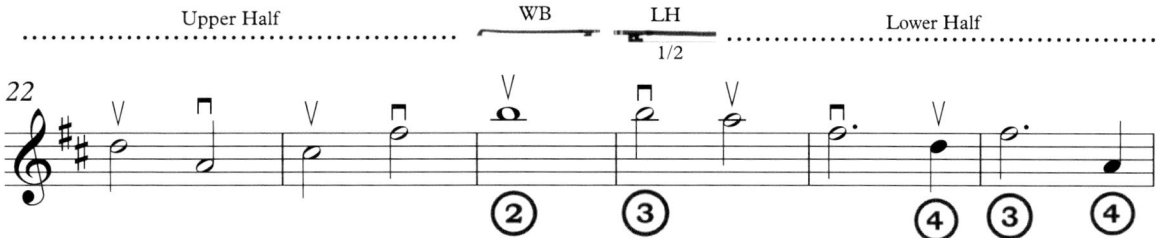
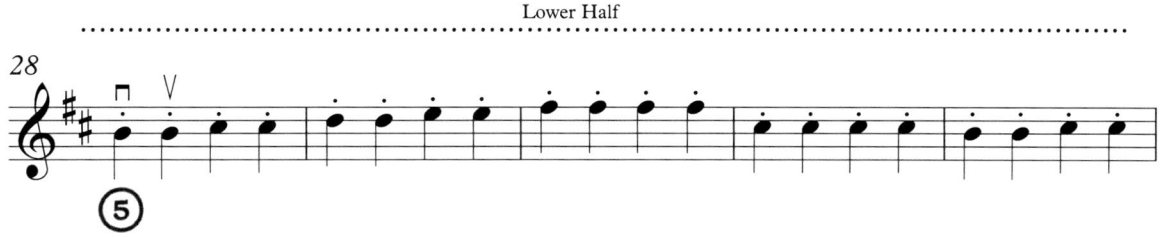
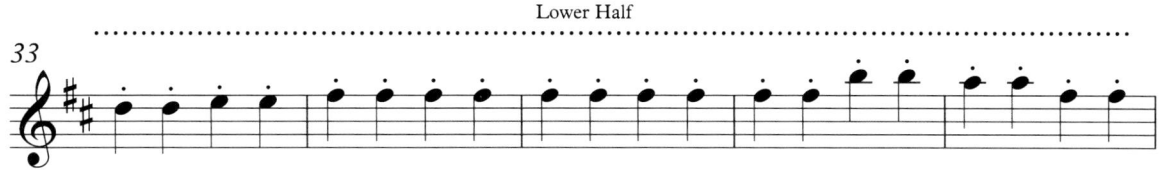
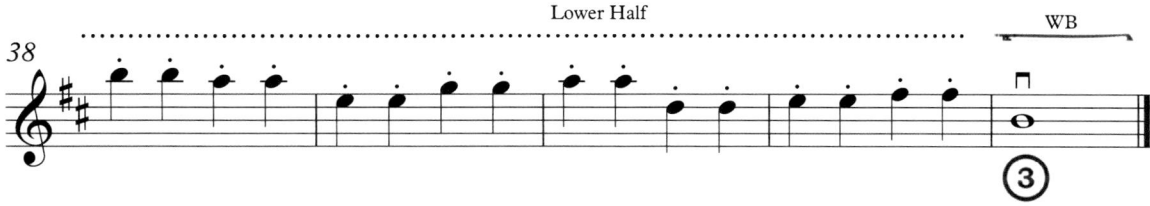

Three

♩ = 100

C.A.

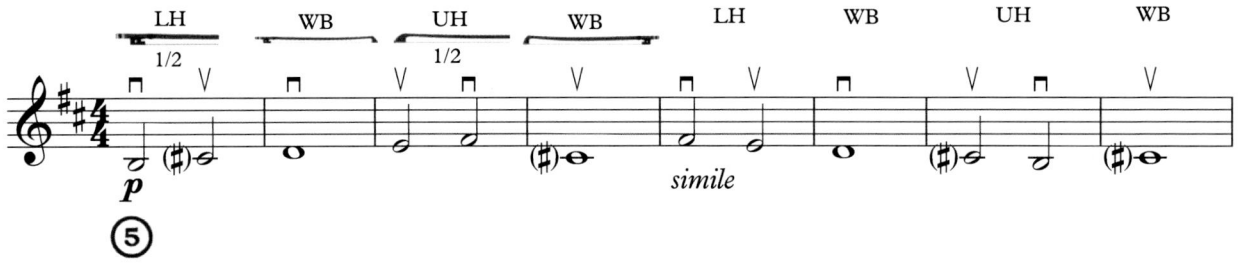
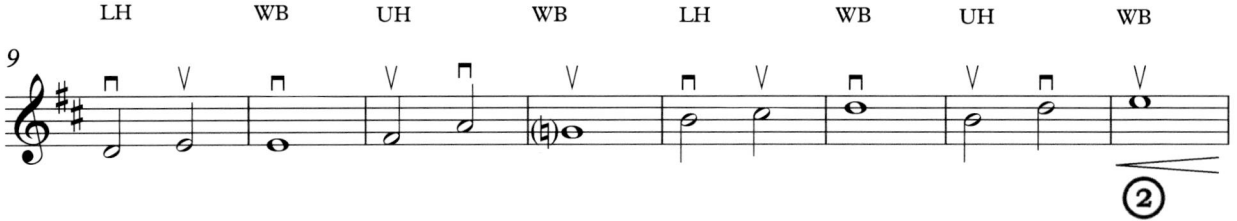
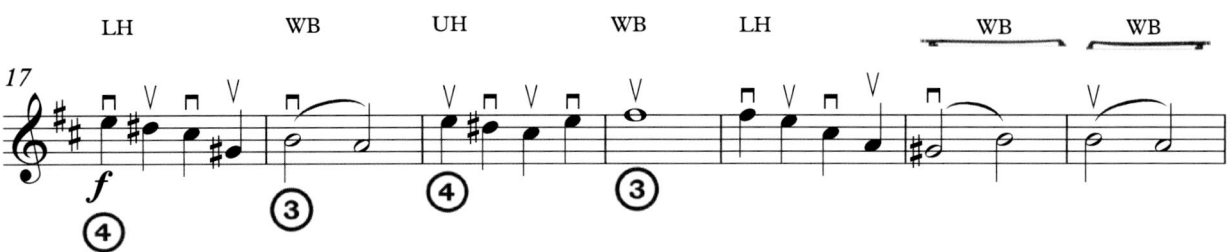
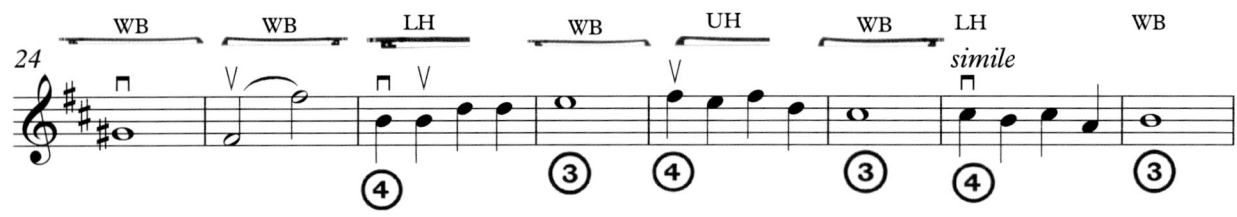

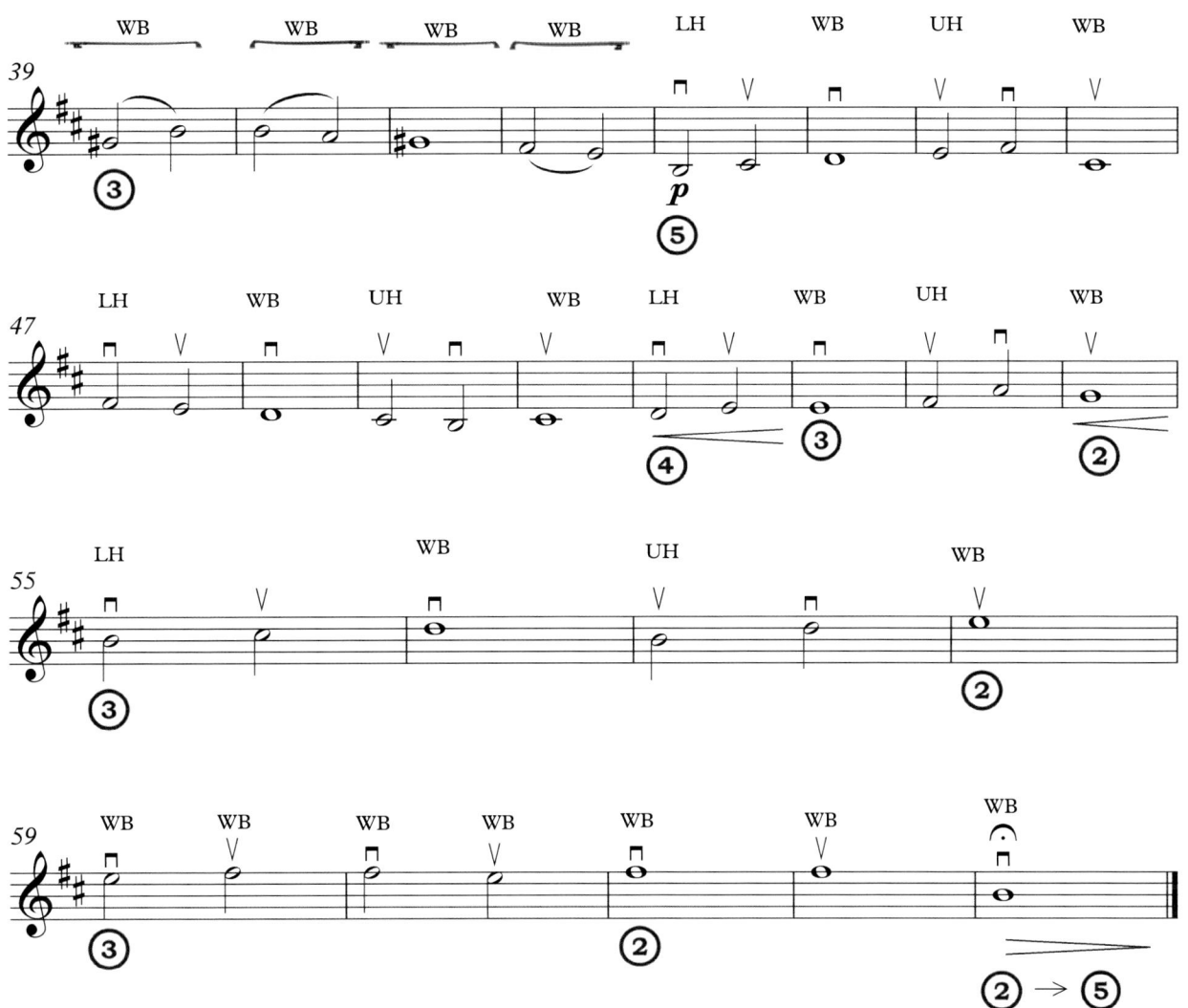

Four

♩ = 80

C.A.

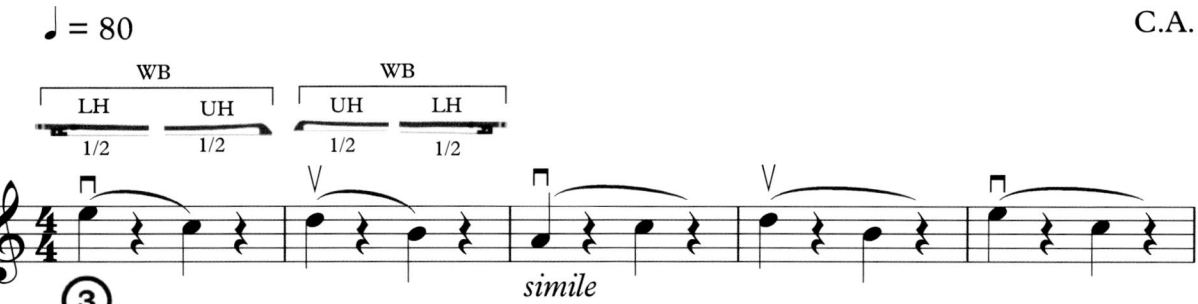

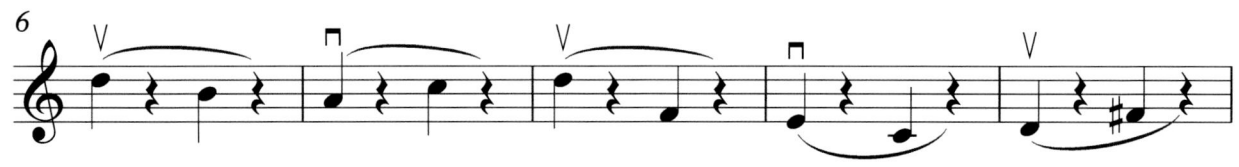

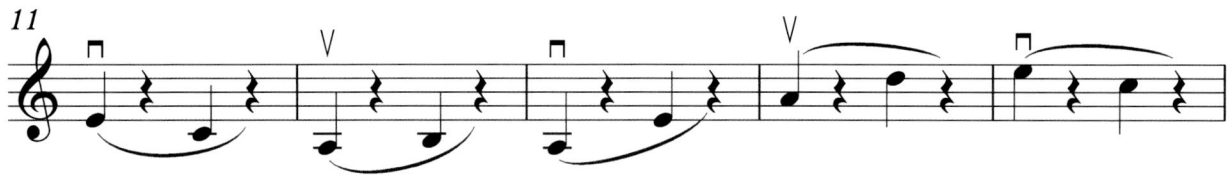

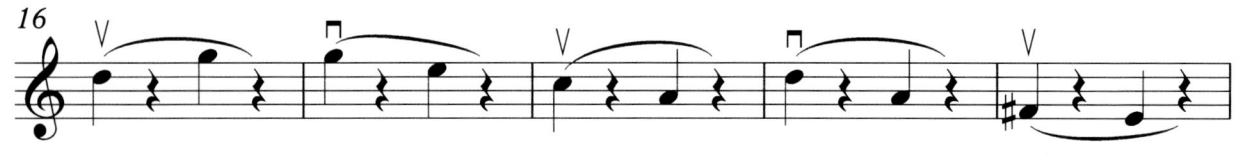

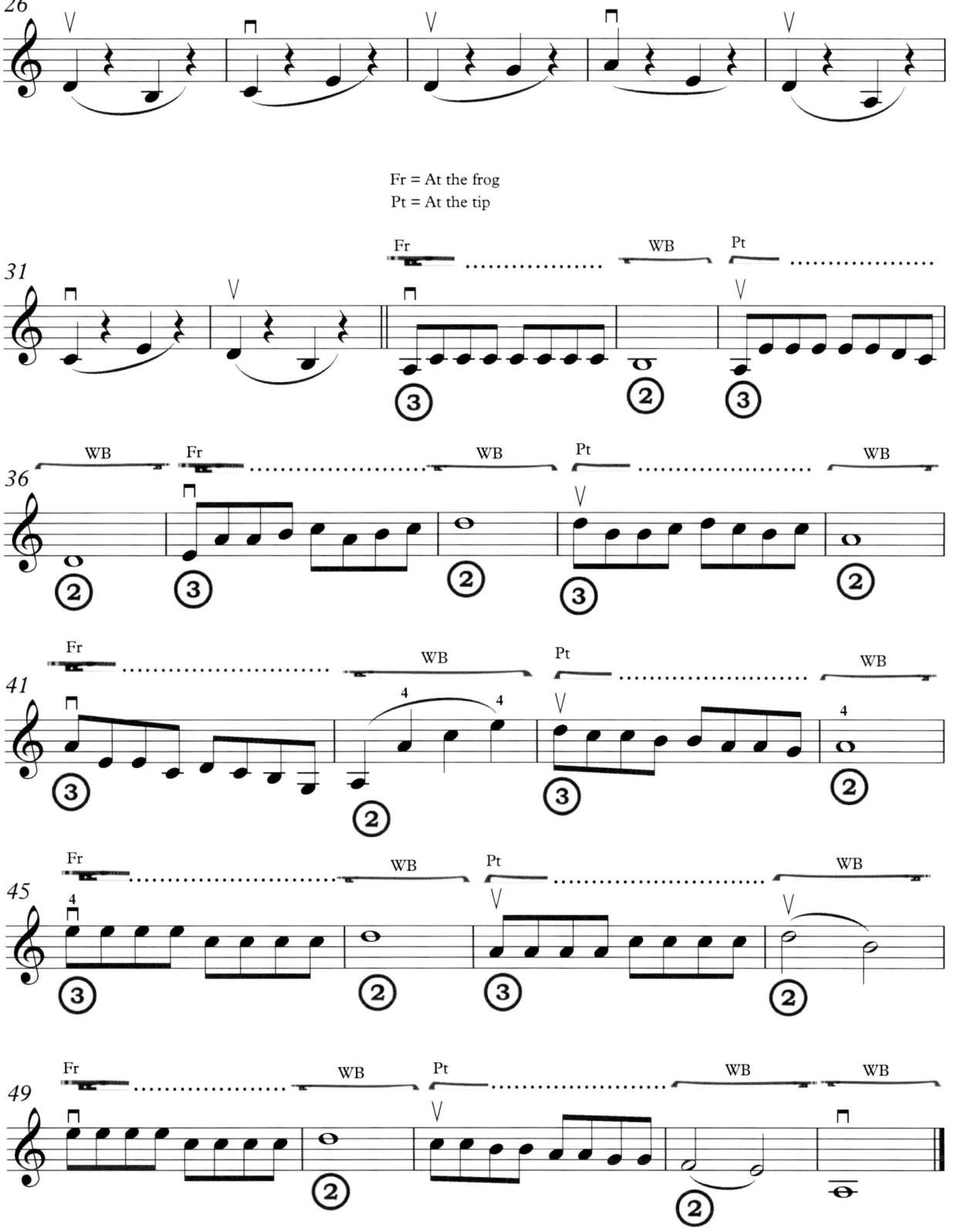

Fr = At the frog
Pt = At the tip

Five

♩ = 75

C.A.

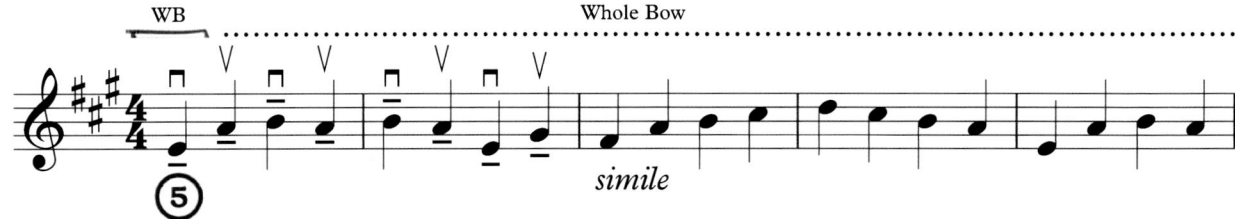

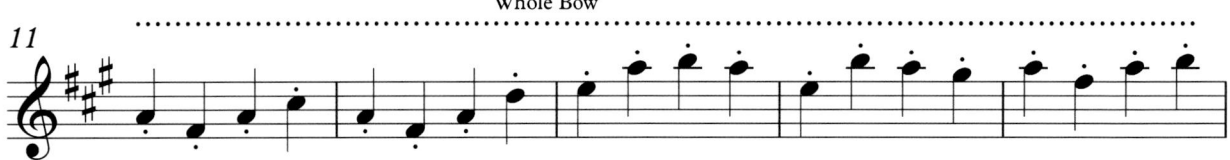

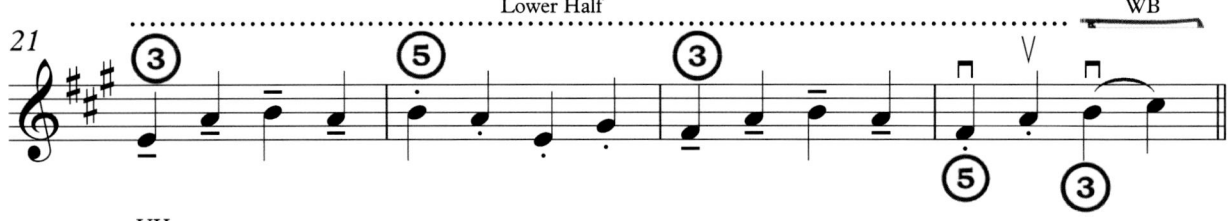
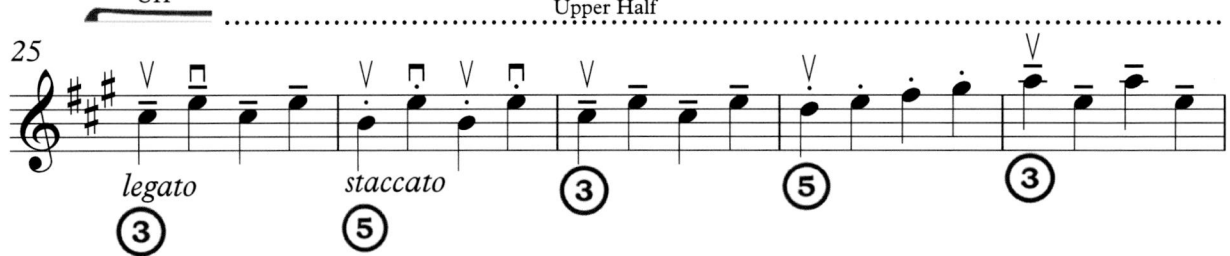

Six

♩ = 90

C.A.

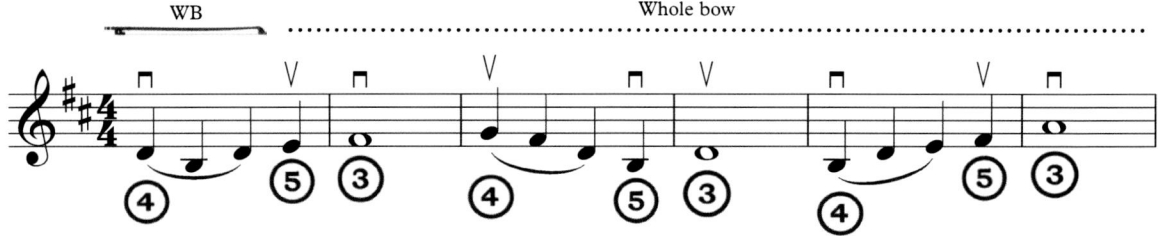
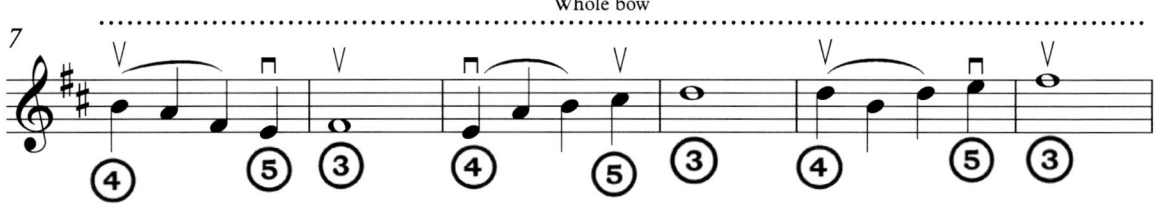
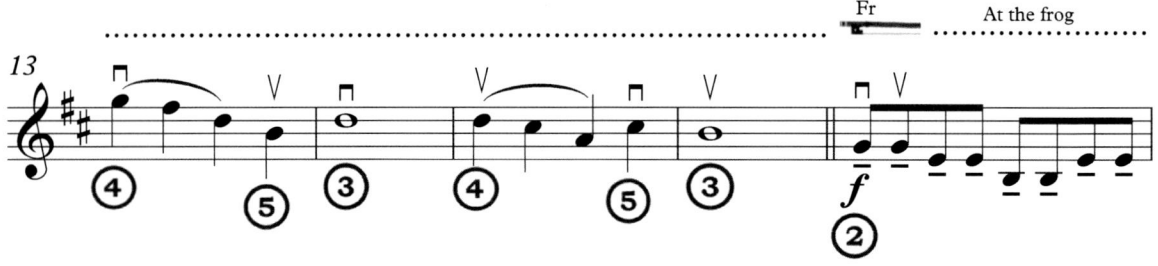

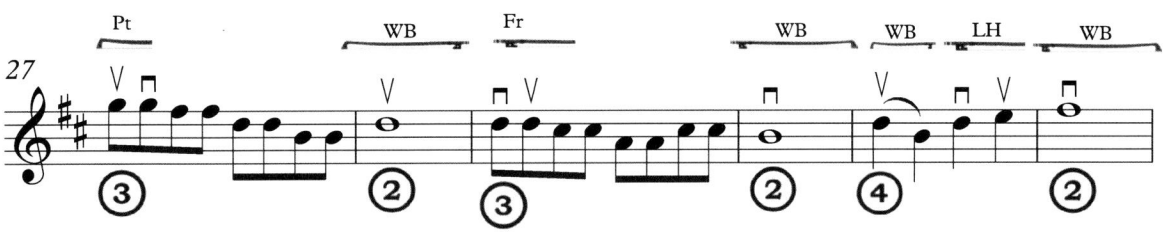
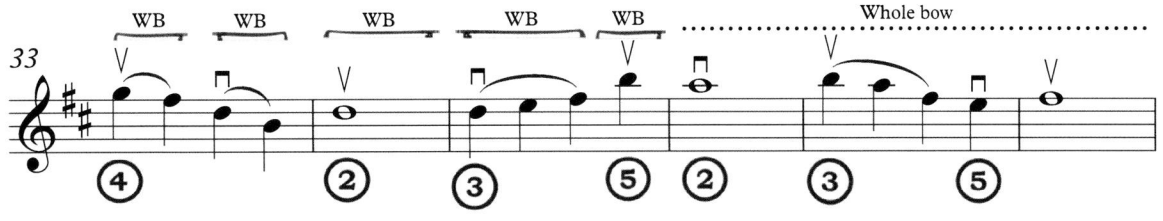
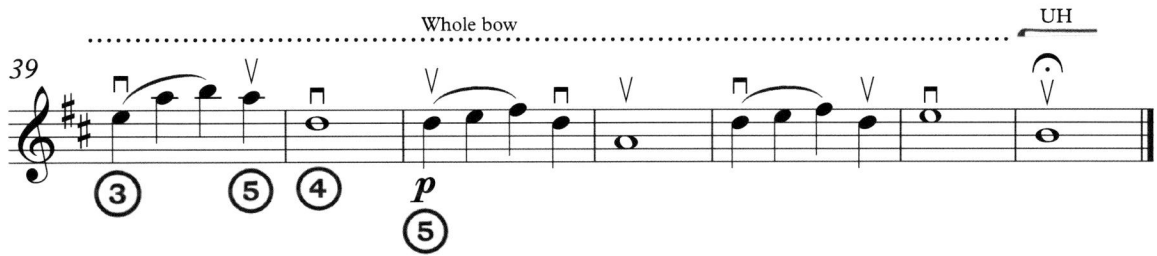

Seven

7

♩ = 80

C.A.

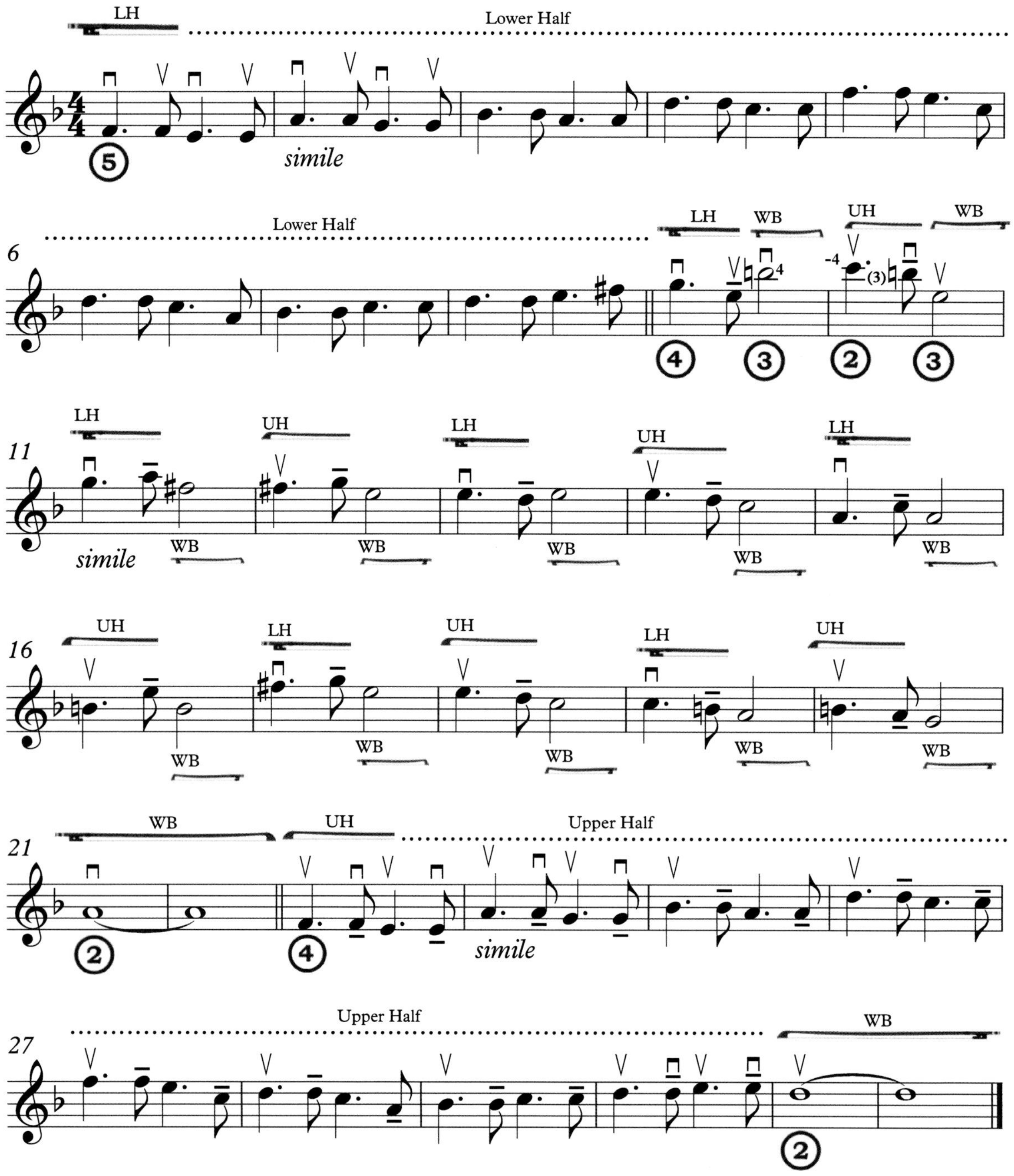
LH
Lower Half
simile
6
Lower Half
LH
WB
UH
WB
11
LH
UH
LH
UH
LH
simile
WB
WB
WB
WB
WB
16
UH
LH
UH
LH
UH
WB
WB
WB
WB
WB
21
WB
UH
Upper Half
simile
27
Upper Half
WB

Pre-Exercise (for Eight)

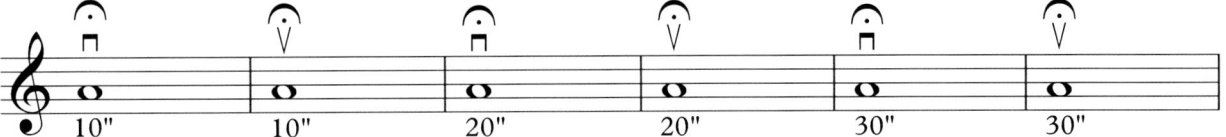

Use the whole bow to sustain a single open string for:

* 10 seconds, then
* 20 seconds, then
* 30 seconds, then
* 40 seconds, then
* 50 seconds, then
* 60 seconds, then

- Track your performance with a timer.

- Aim for a clean, steady and beautiful sound.

- Stay near the bridge (①, ②)

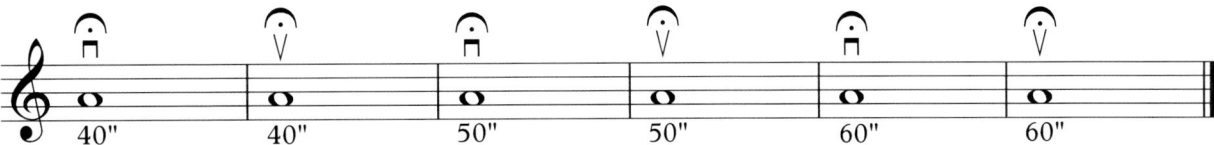

Even if the sound sometimes stops or scratches, this exercise will bring tremendous benefits.

Your general bow control and tone production will improve.

Eight

♩ = 80

C.A.

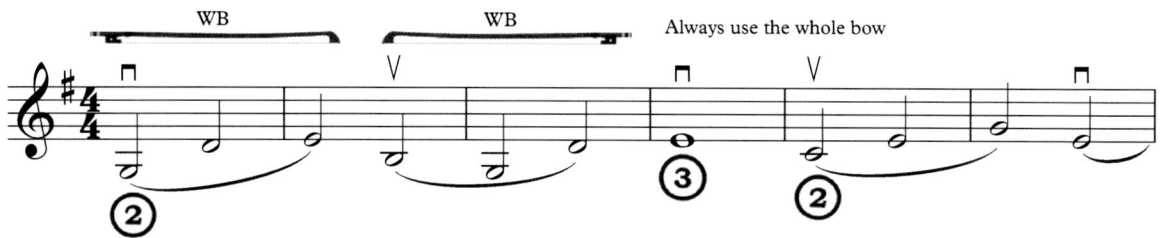

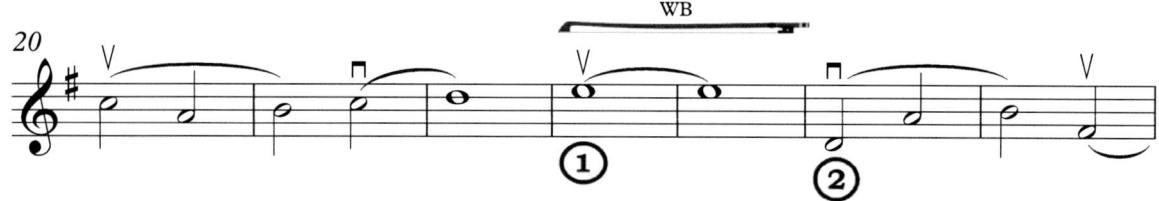

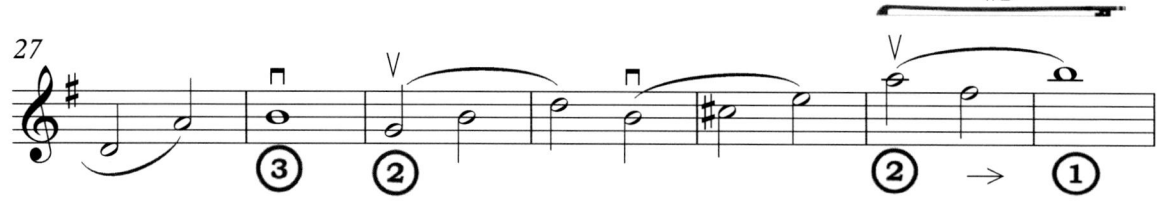

Nine

♩ = 80

C.A.

Ten

♩ = 90

C.A.

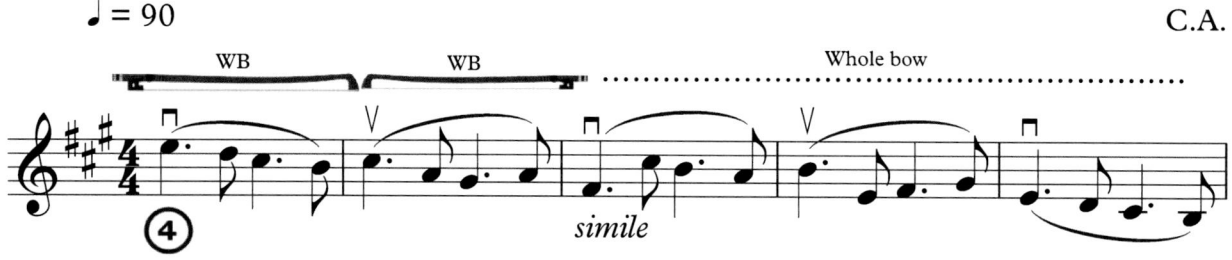
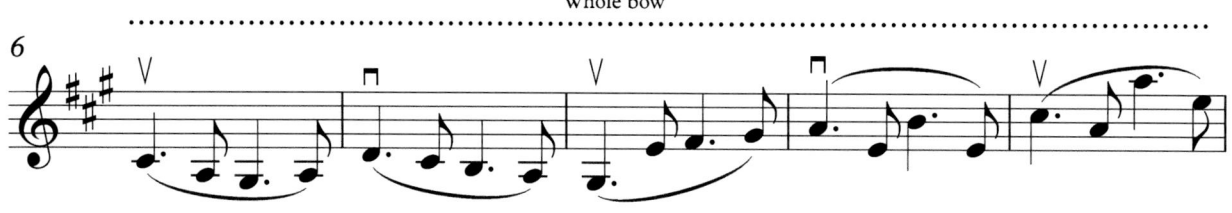
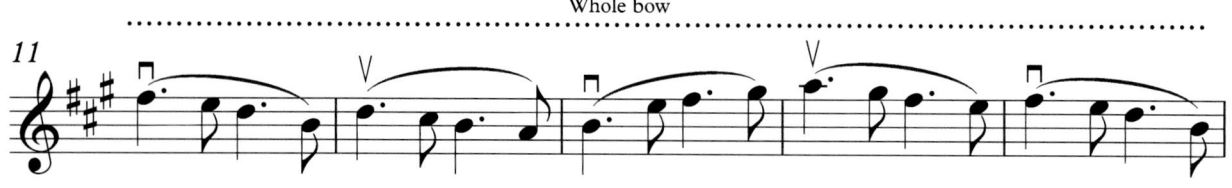
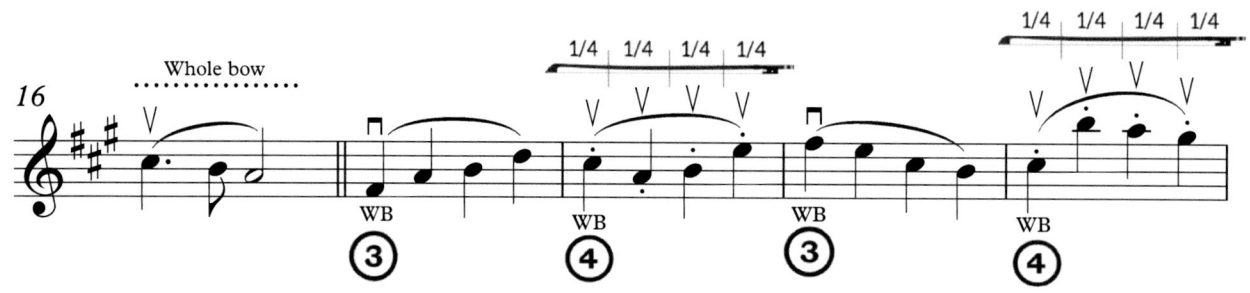

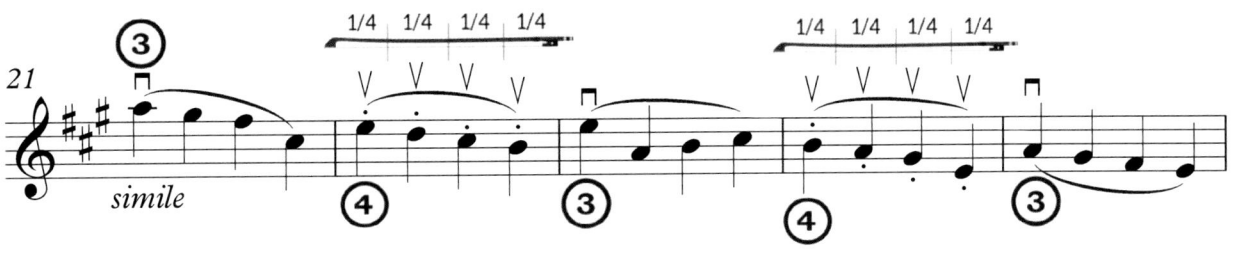
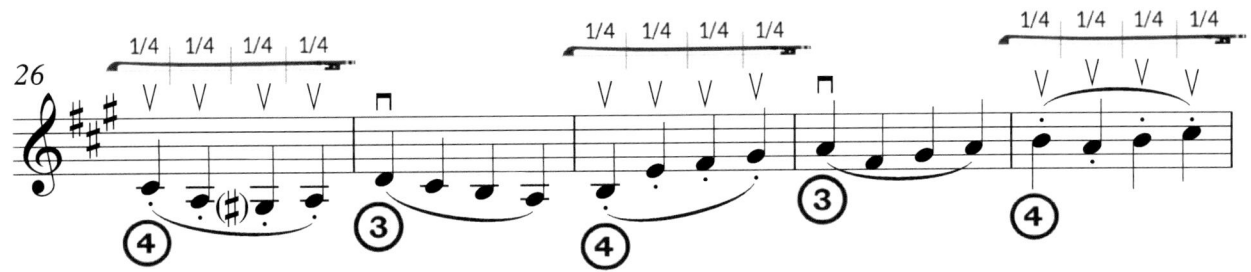
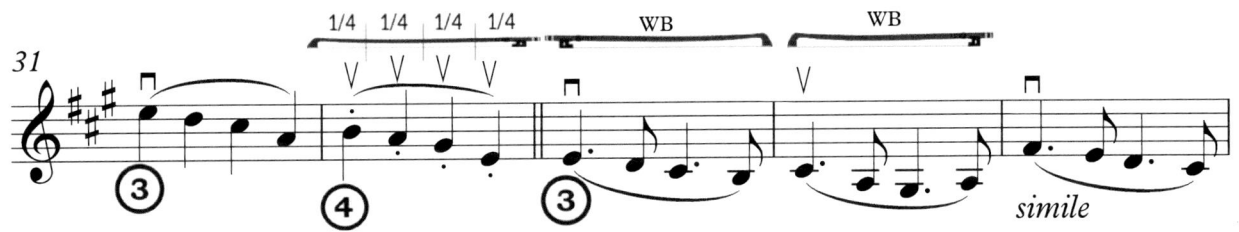

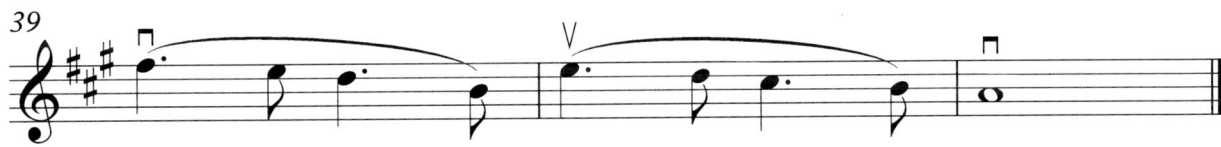

Eleven A

♩ = 90

C.A.

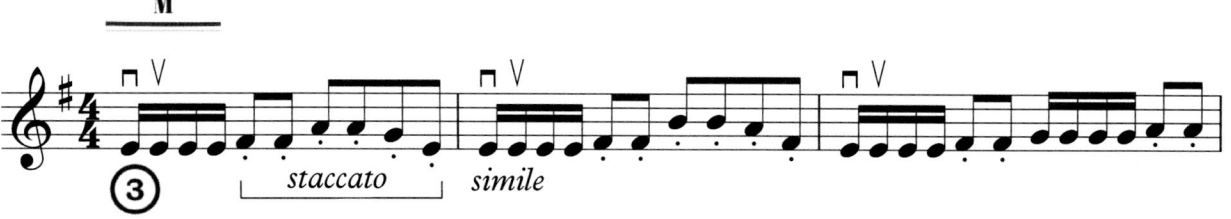

23

Eleven B

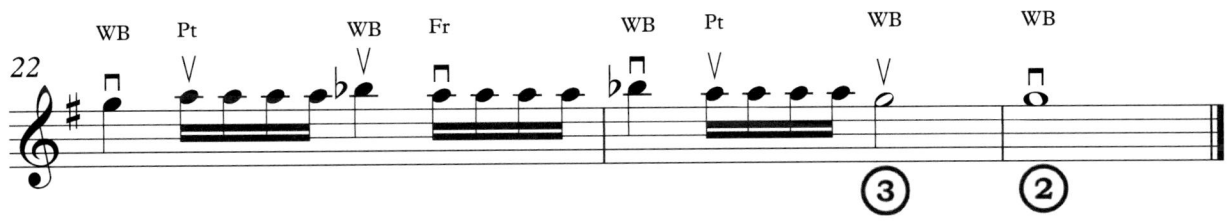

Twelve

♩ = 115

C.A.

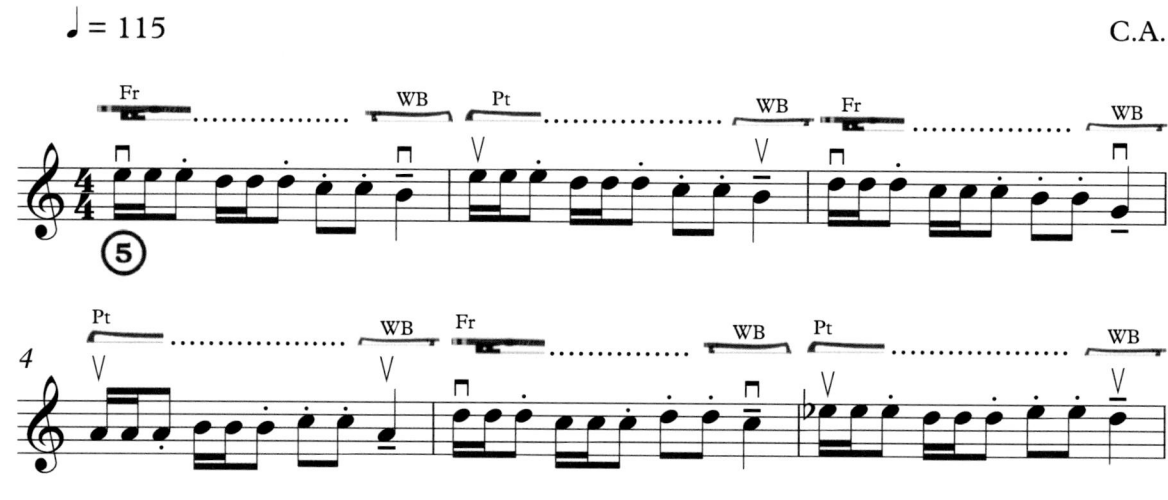

Thirteen

C.A.

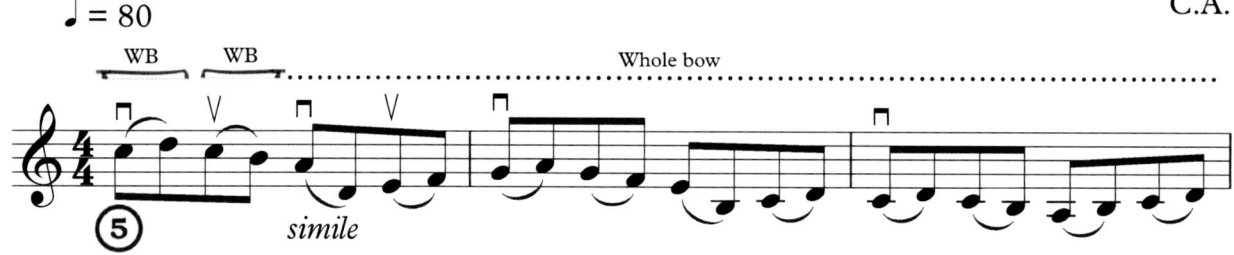
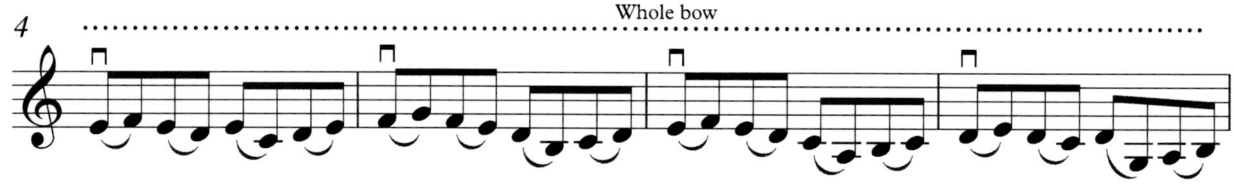
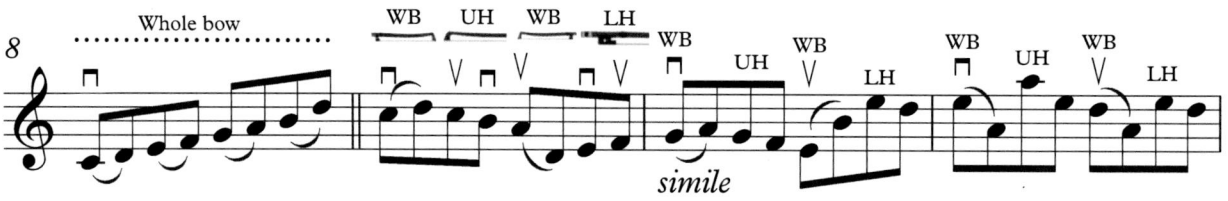
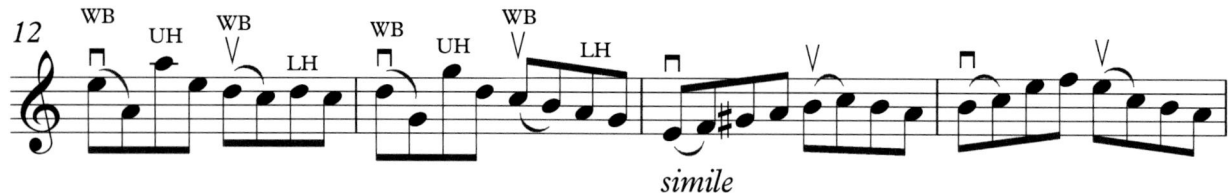
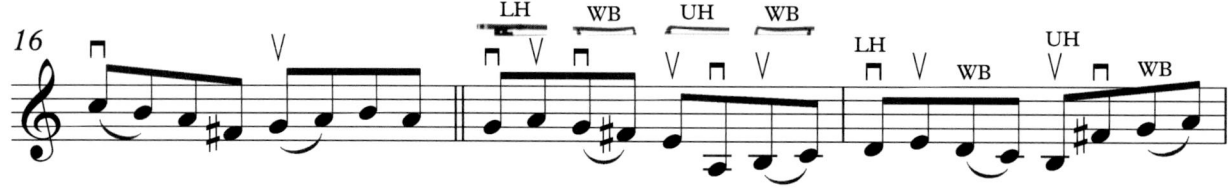
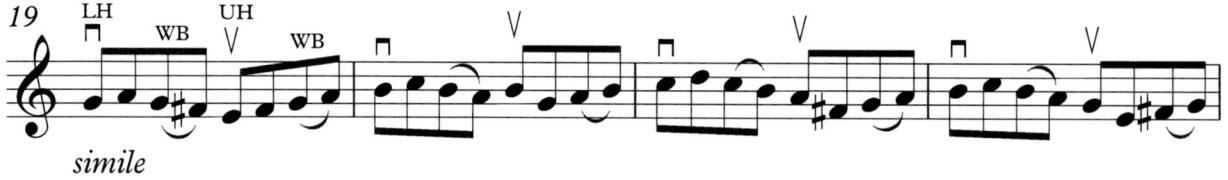

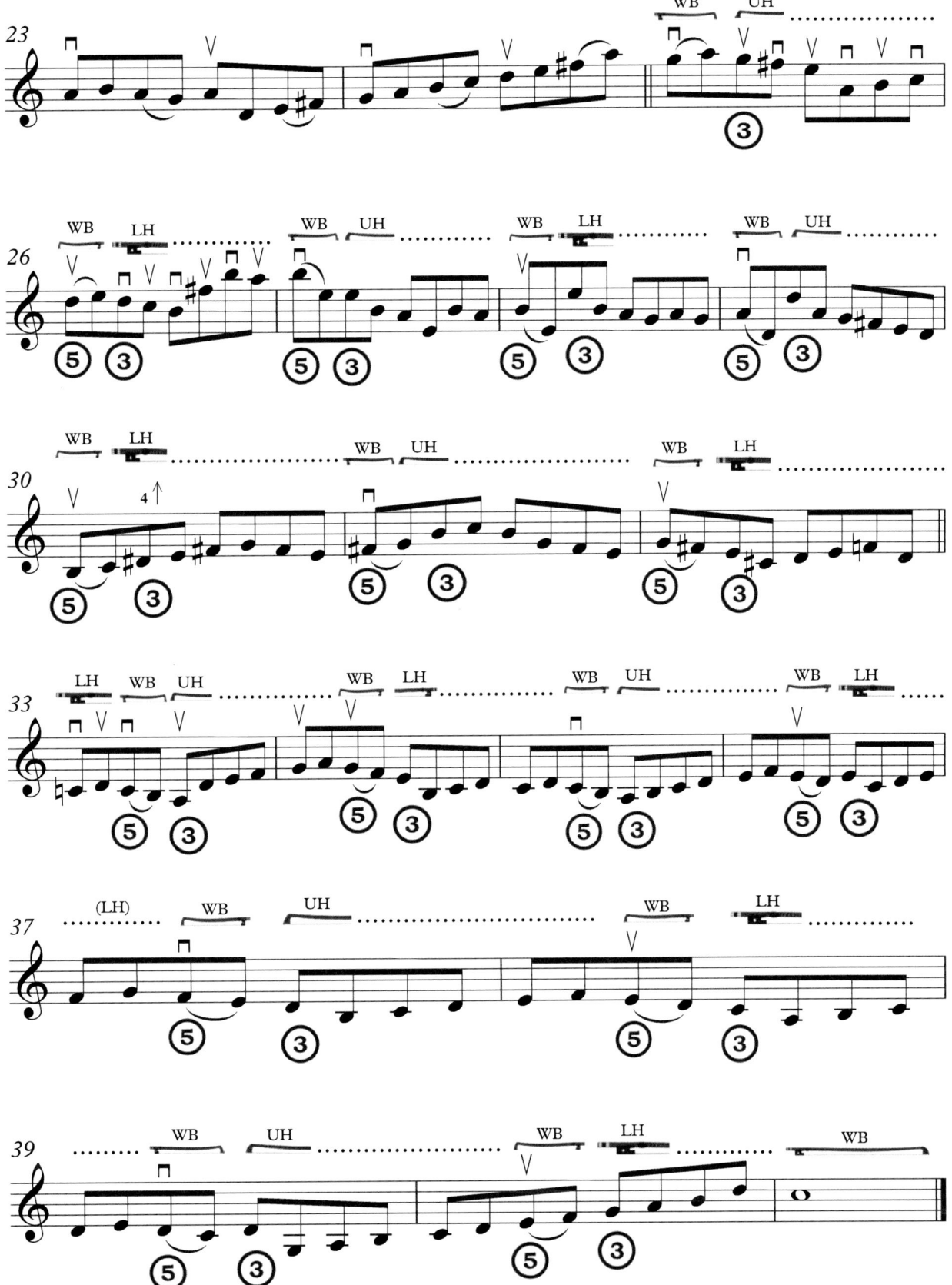

Fourteen

♪ = 120

C.A.

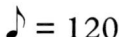
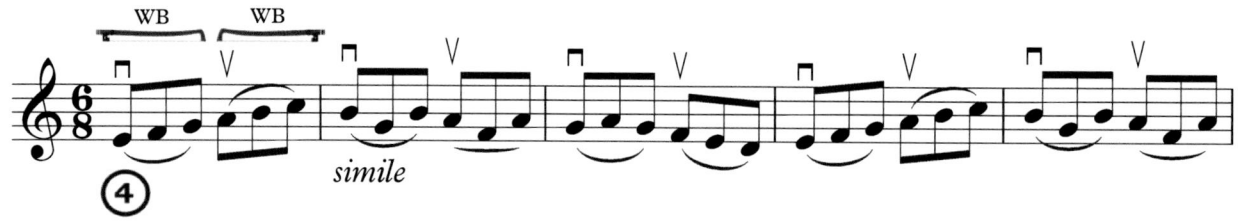

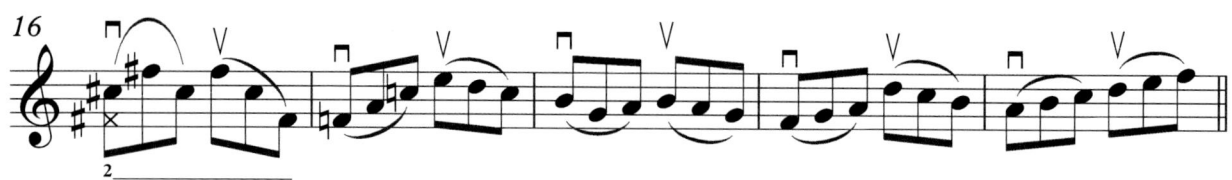
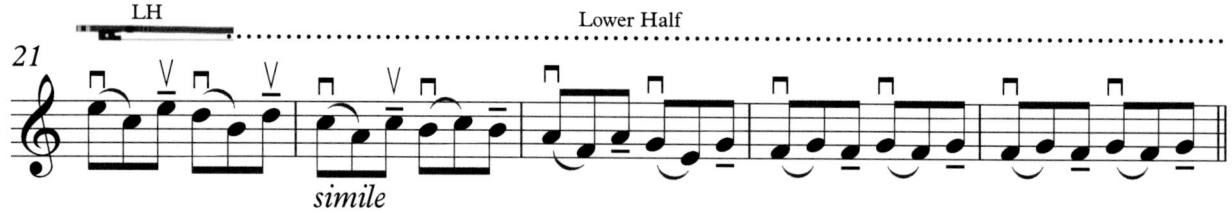

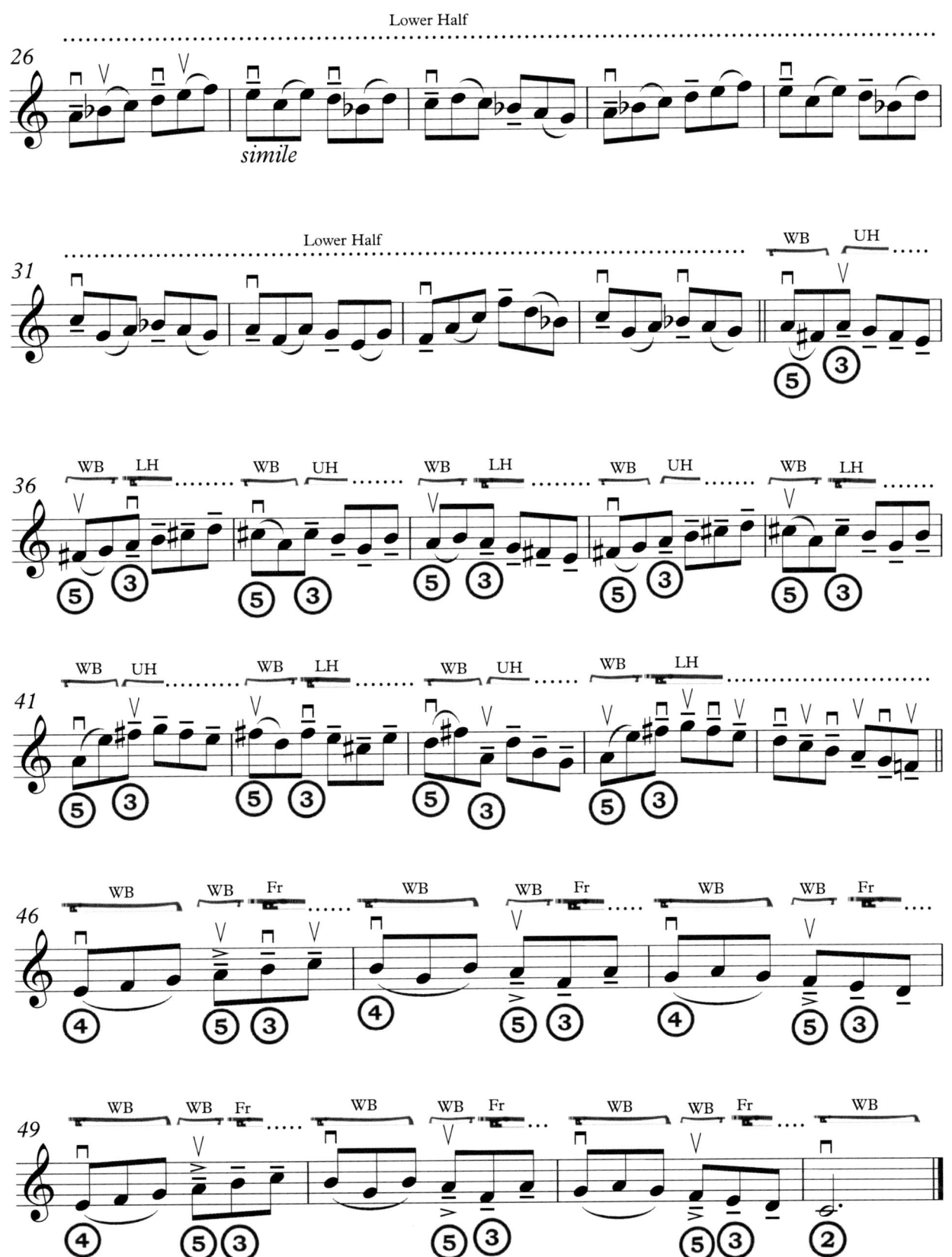

Fifteen

♪ = 110

C.A.

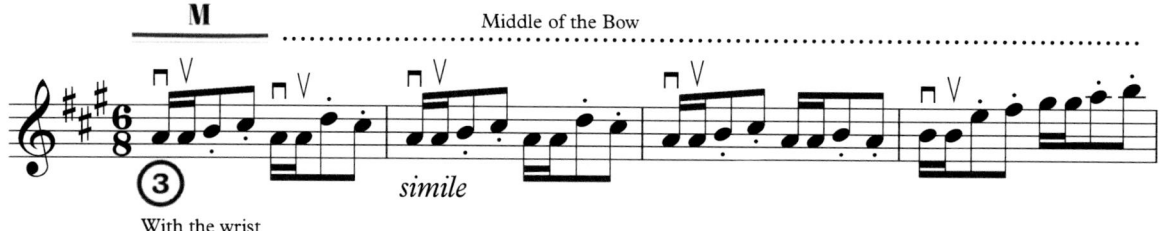

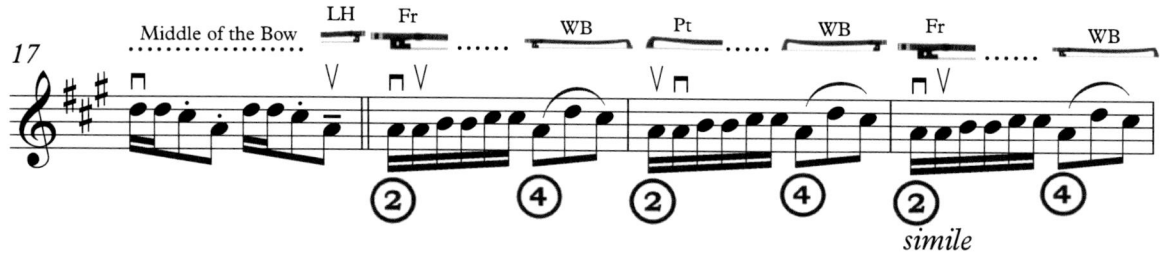

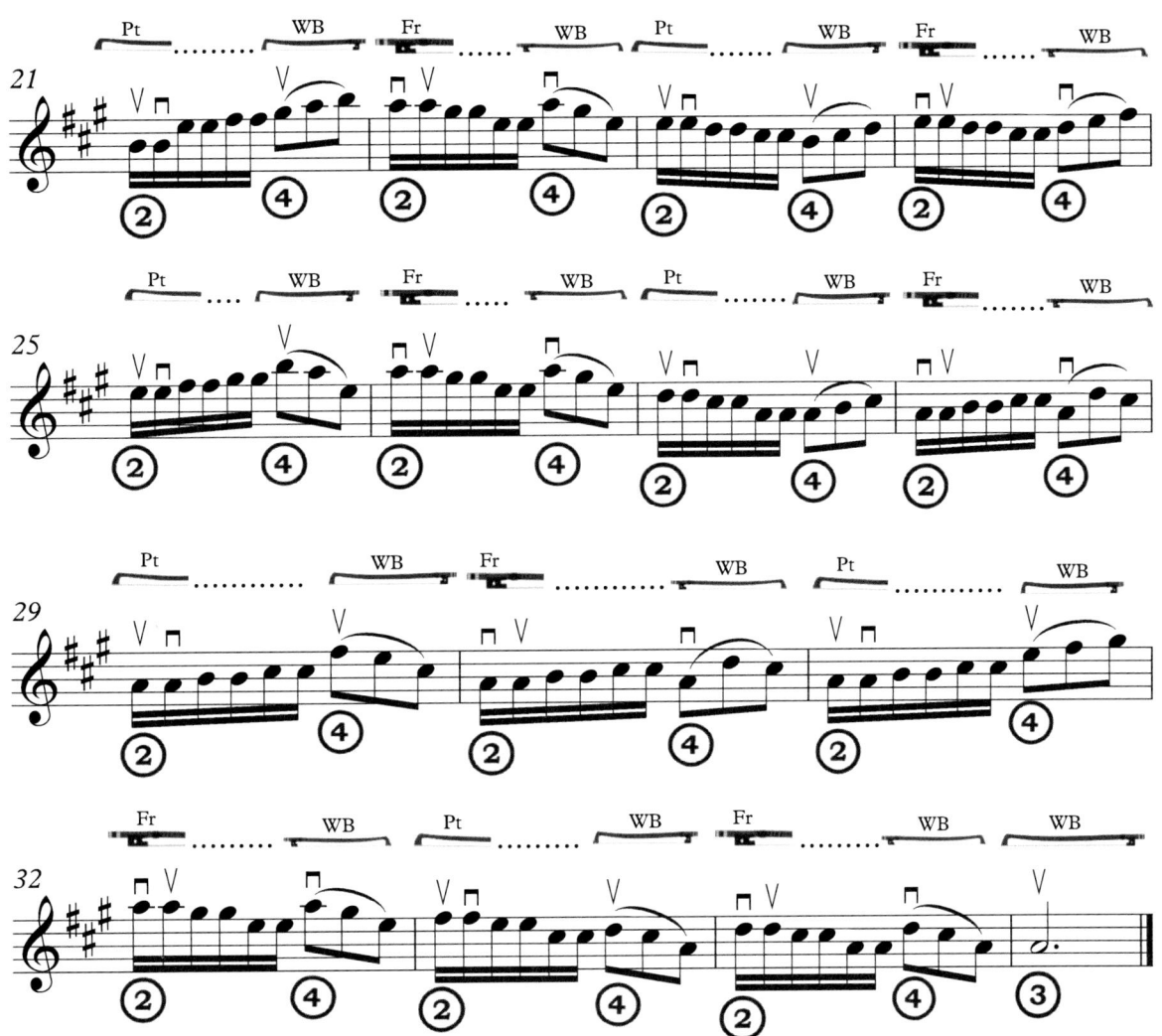

Sixteen

♪ = 120

C.A.

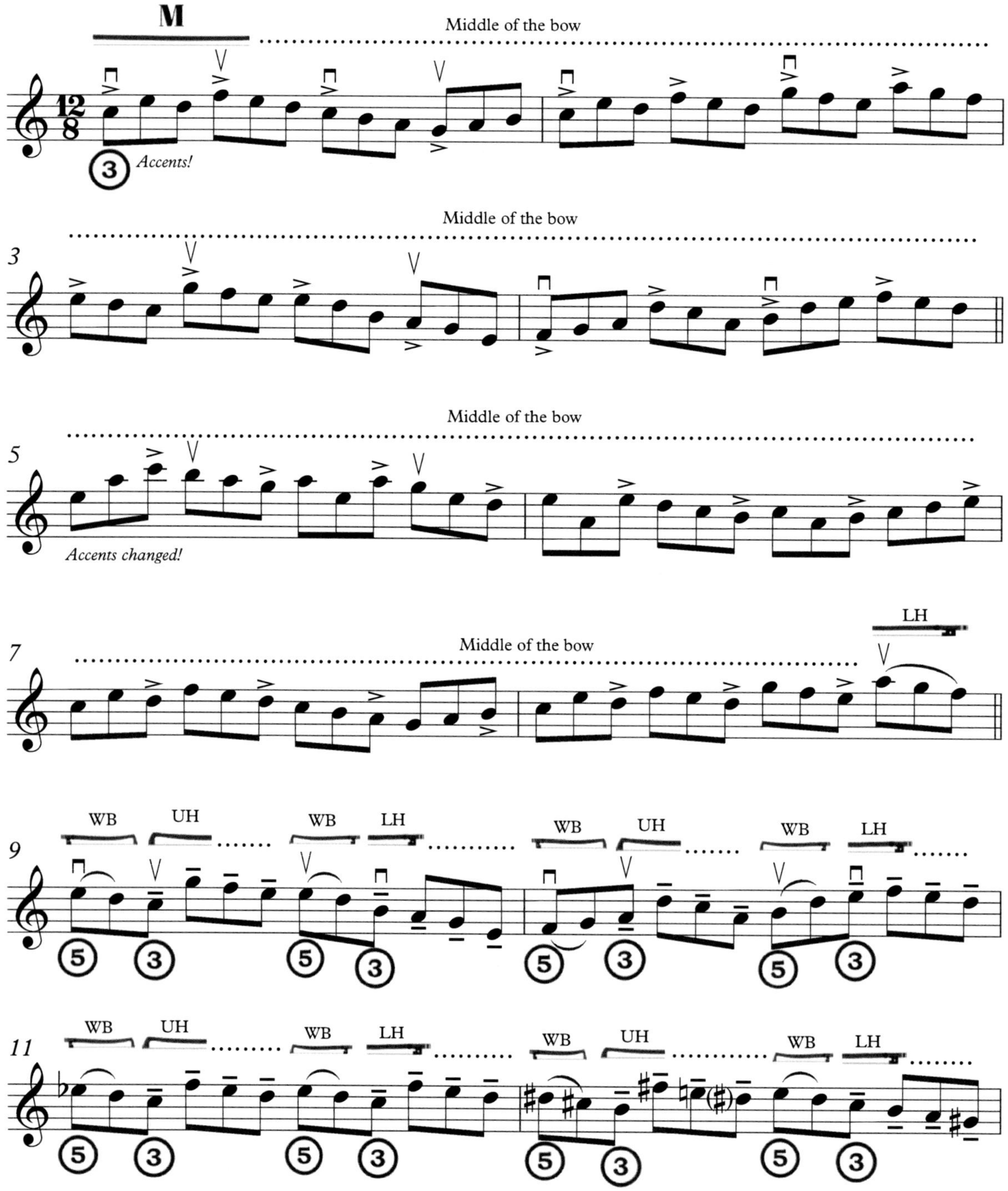

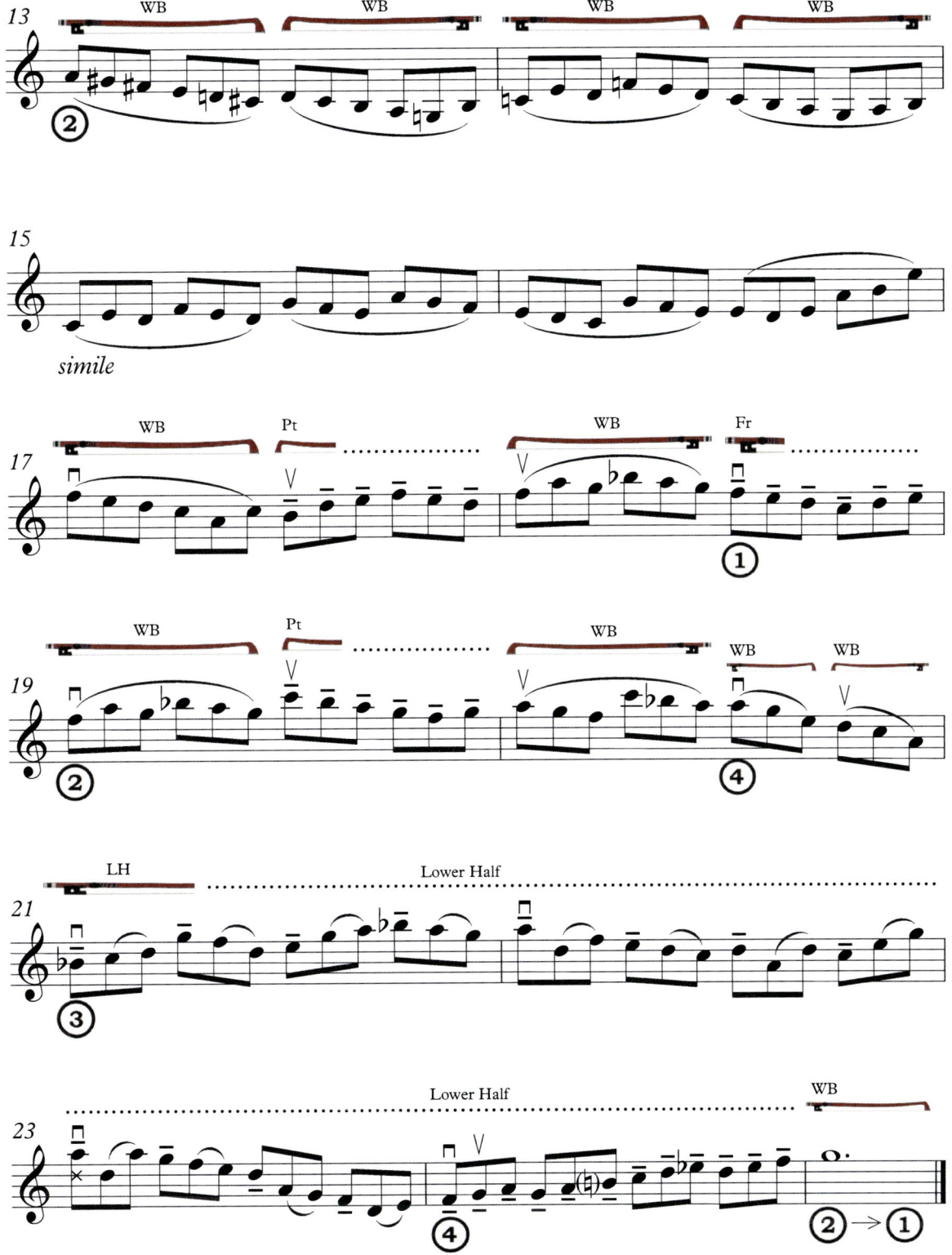

Seventeen

C.A.

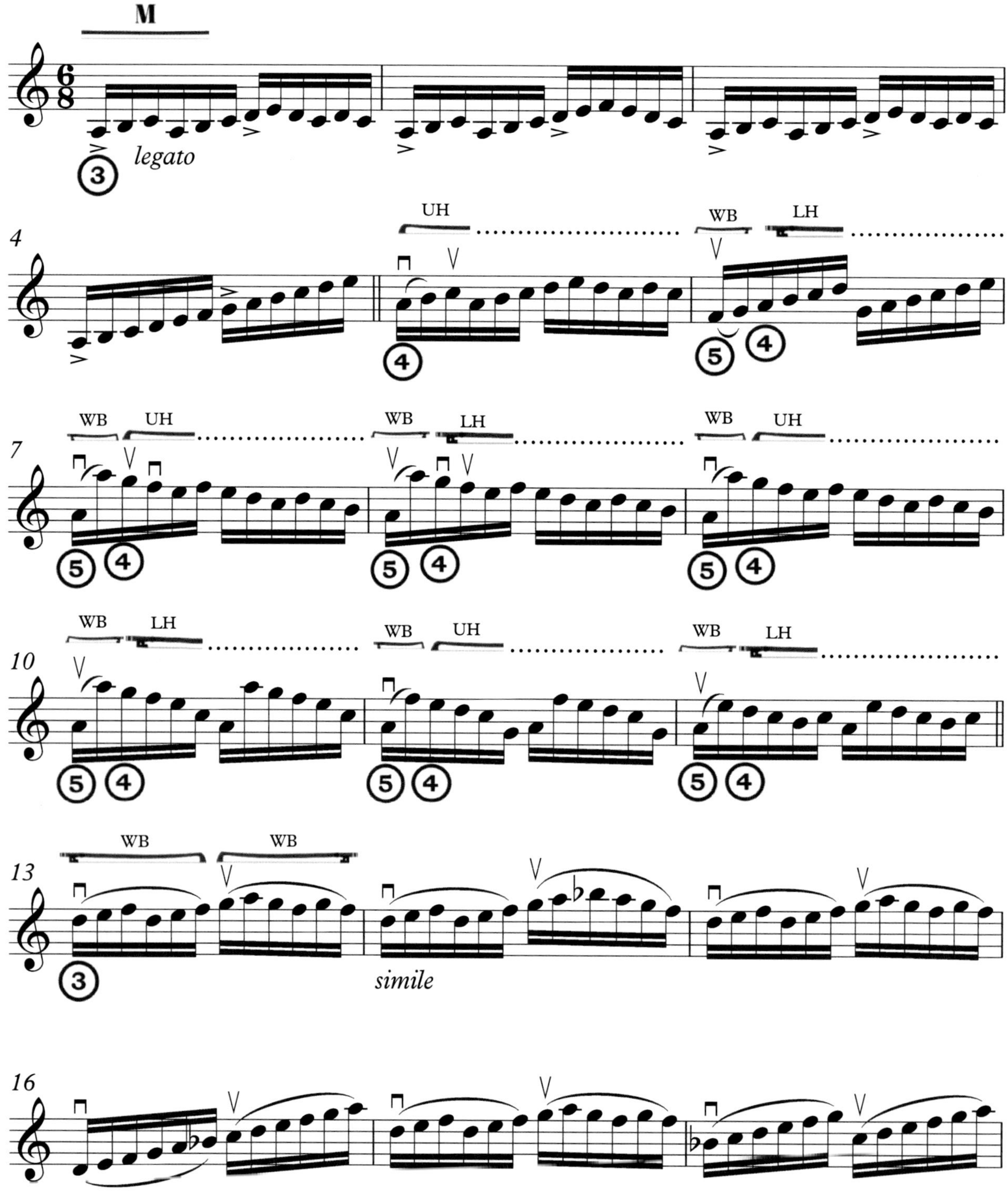

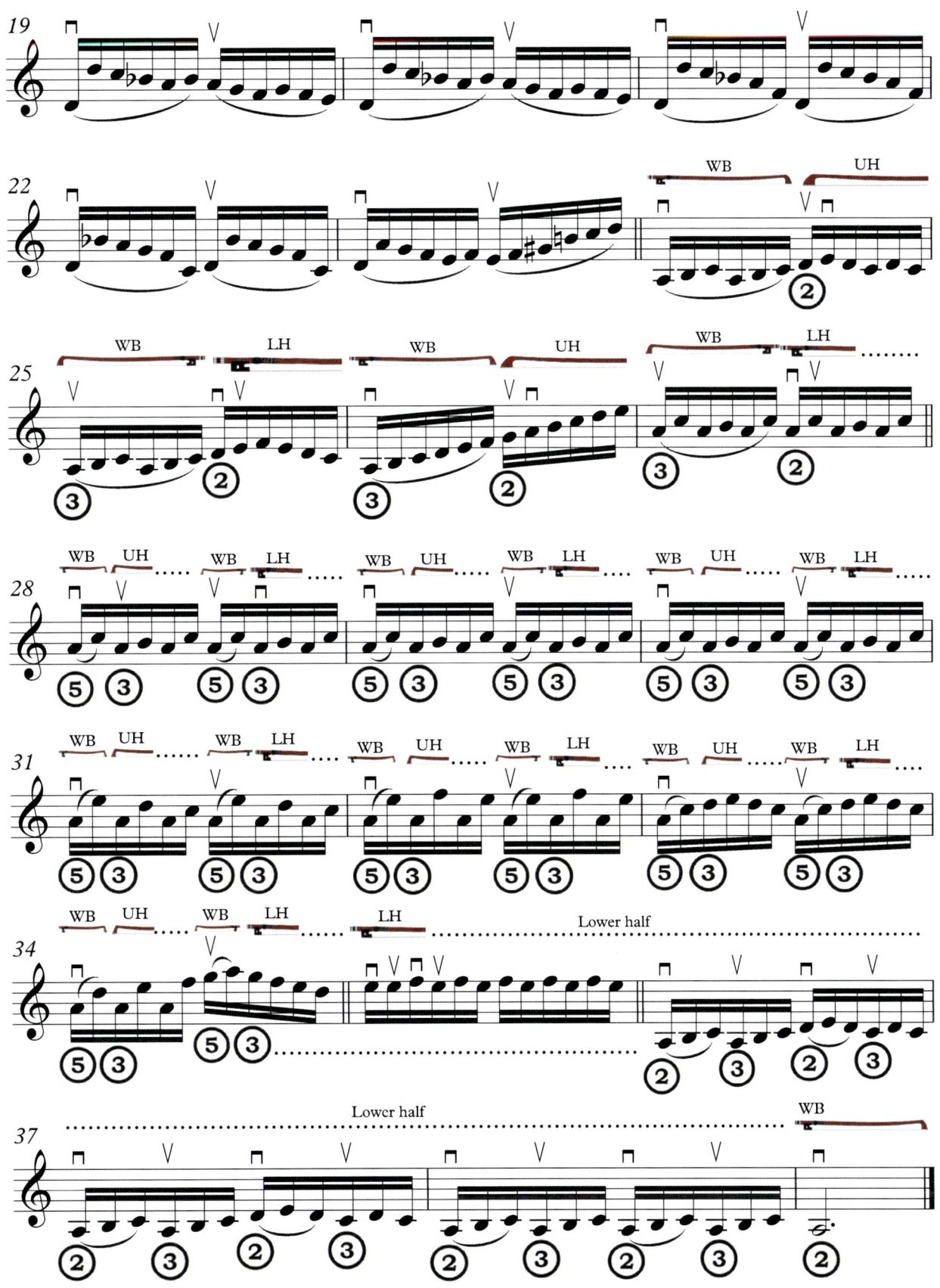

Eighteen

18

♩ = 90

C.A.

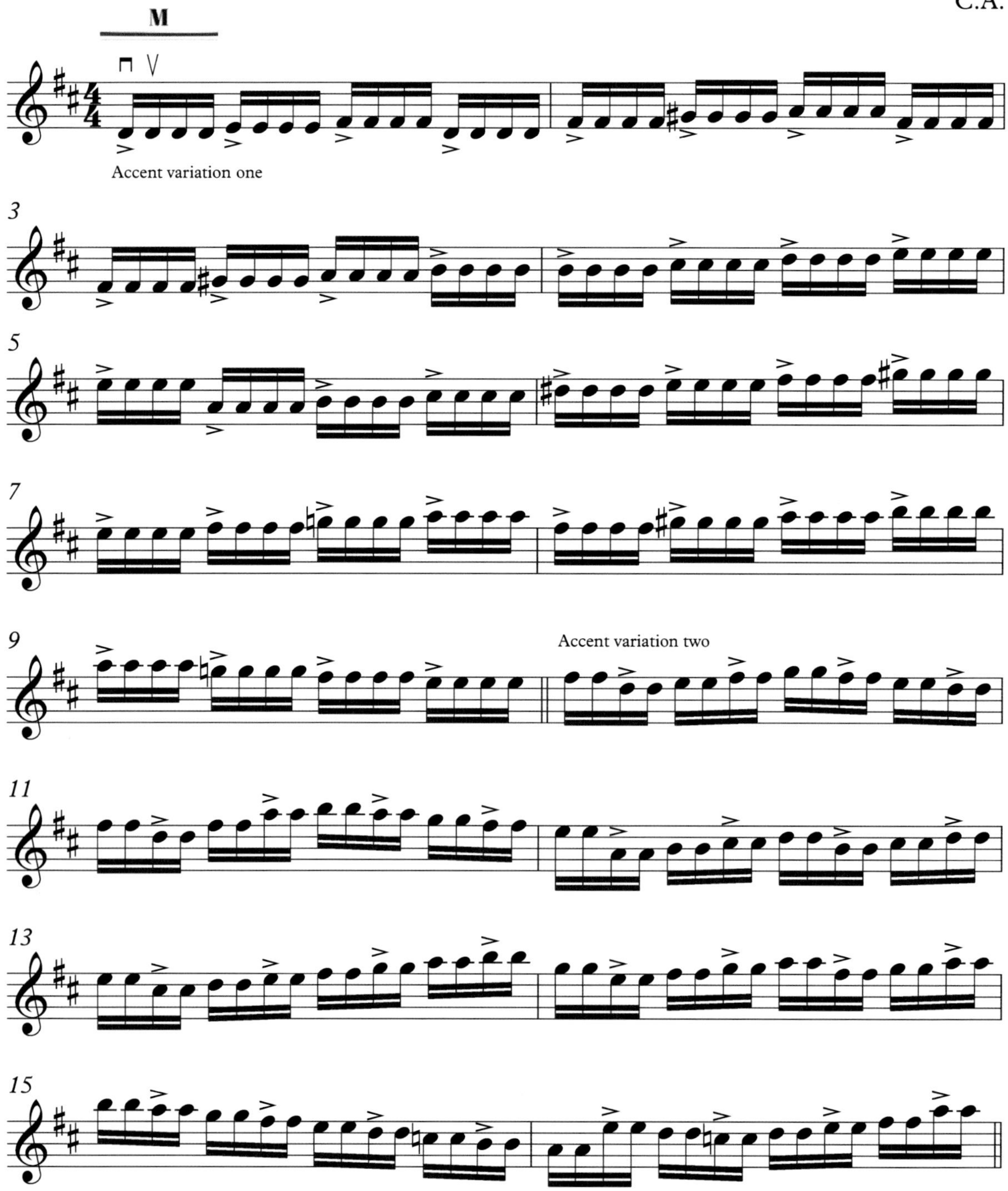
M
Accent variation one
3
5
7
9
Accent variation two
11
13
15

Practice on contact points:

② ③ ④

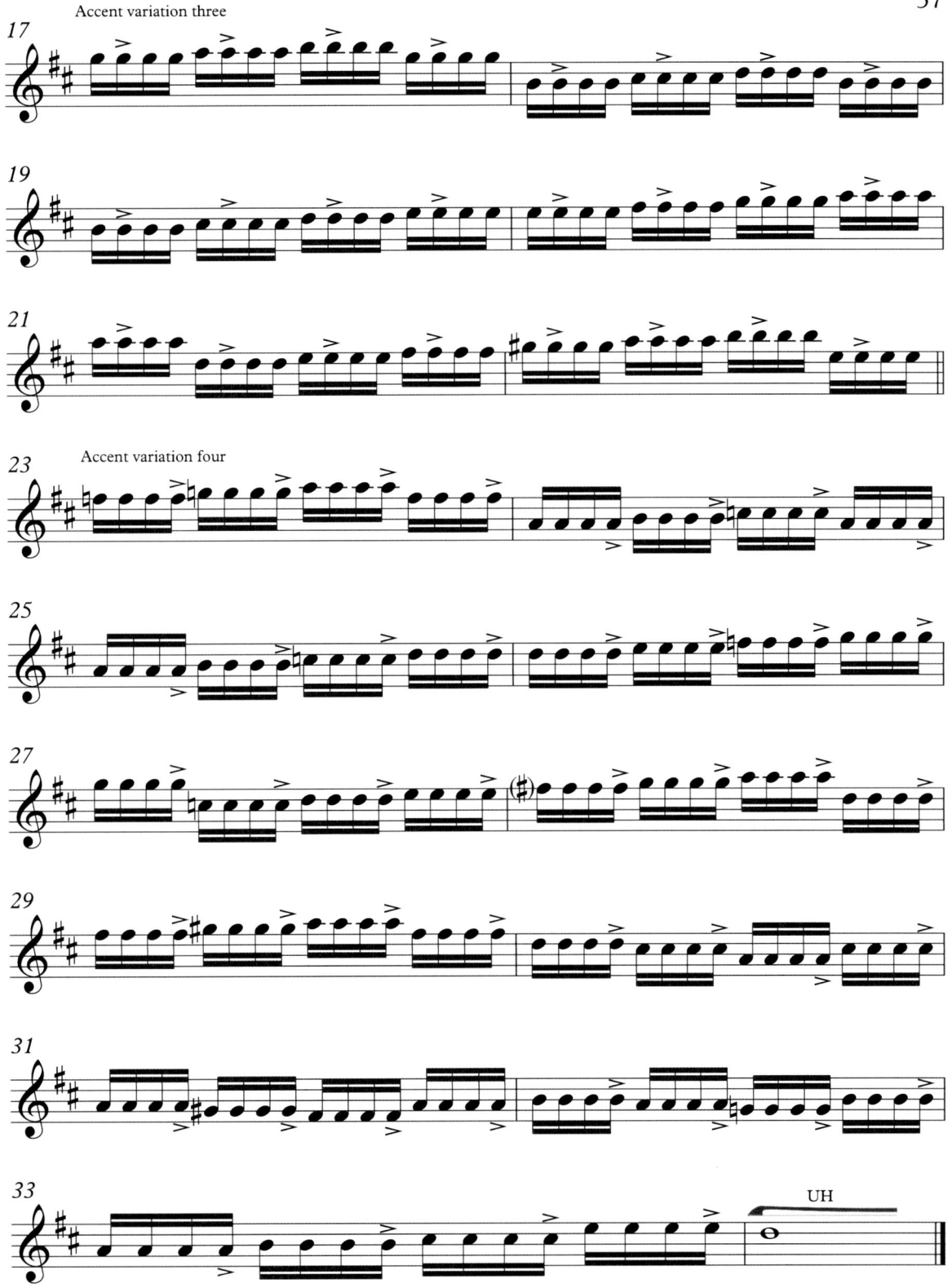

Nineteen

♩ = 60

C.A.

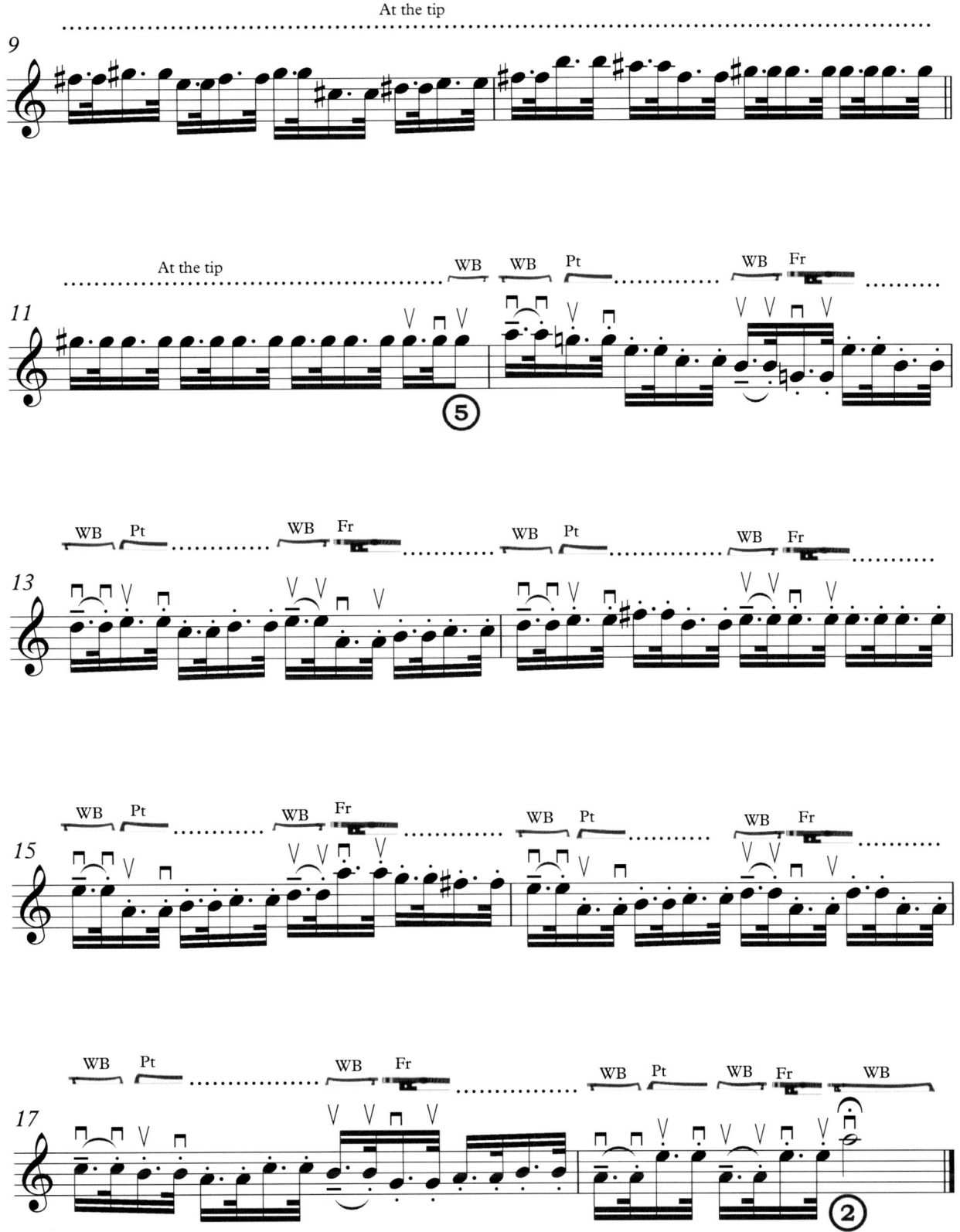

Twenty

♩ = 90

C.A.

41

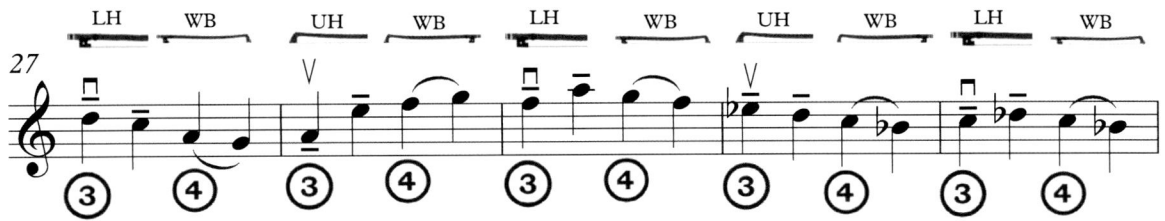
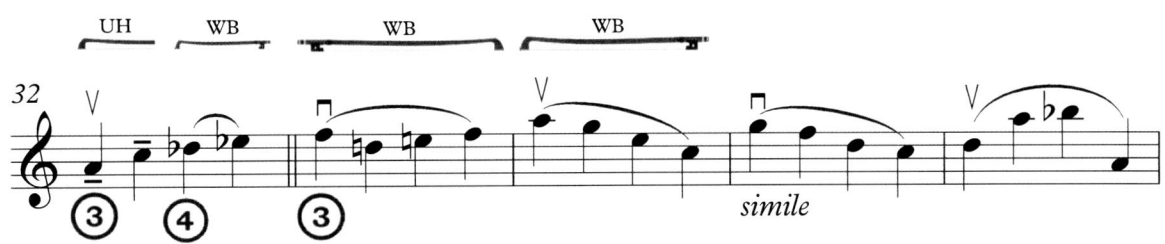
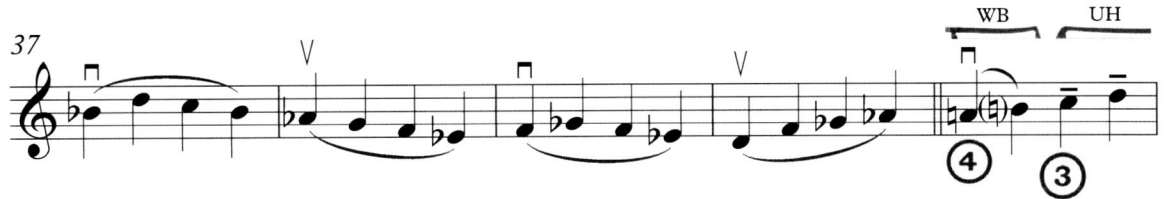
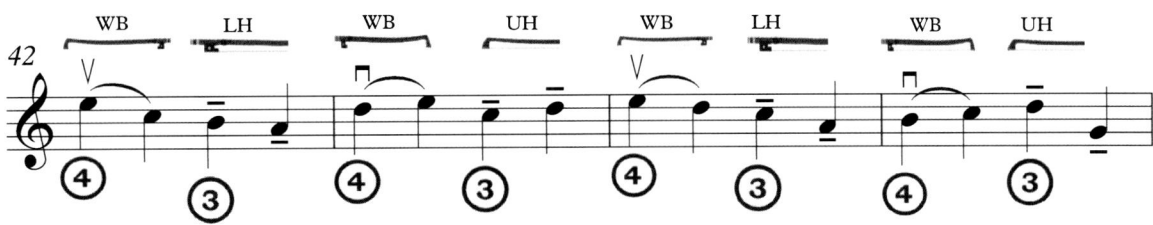

Notes

Notes

Notes

Notes

Notes

Notes

About the Author

Puerto Rican violinist and composer César Avilés holds a Master's degree from the University of New Mexico as well as a Bachelor's degree from the Conservatory of Music of Puerto Rico in Violin Performance and Composition. César also studied instrumental composition and film music at Berklee. His concert compositions have been performed in Europe as well as in North and South America. He is working on a quest to visit 50 countries and experience the world's top 20 orchestras live. With his family, César lives near Cologne, Germany, where he serves as violin and string orchestra teacher at the Musikschule Düren.

Also Available by César Avilés

Studies expertly written as an intensive course in learning the basics of the third position.

An exciting continuation of Vol.I covering advanced fingerings and extensions in the third position.

www.stringorchestrasheetmusic.com

Password for online resources:

bowingpatterns1324

Motivation is not reliable.
Don't count on it. Instead, start working on what's important to you.
Even if it's for a minute. You'll create momentum.
And eventually, build the habit of showing up daily,
which I believe is the fastest way to improve anything.
It may also be the hardest part of the craft.

© 2019 by César Avilés
www.stringorchestrasheetmusic.com

Made in the USA
Coppell, TX
25 October 2019